Diabetic Smoothie Recipe Book:

Healthy and Easy Diabetic Smoothie Diet.

By

Victoria Stone

Hi!

Thank you for purchasing our book. Your support and trust in us are much appreciated. **Use this QR code to get an electronic variant of this book as a GIFT from us**! No more will cookbooks be ruined with unsightly splodges or splashes of cooking sauces, with our e-version.

How to use the book?

In each recipe you can see a QR code. After scanning this code, you will see a photo of the finished dish.

Why do we use QR codes in our books?

1) It is modern, innovative, and eco-friendly.

2) It saves book production costs, reduces energy, paint, and paper costs. This is our contribution to the care of the planet and the environment.

3) All this allows us to make the price of the book lower for buyers. Plus, you get not only the paperback, but also the electronic version of the book absolutely for free!

4) Thank you for contributing to the care of the environment with us!

Table of Contents

Introduction

Are you a smoothie lover? Do you want to try the healthiest of the low-carb and diabetic friendly smoothies? Now you have a whole list of options to try a smoothie from! This cookbook brings you 50 rich and delicious diabetic smoothie recipes that are super quick and easy to make. All the recipes are created using low-carb veggies and sugar-free ingredients to keep your glucose levels under control. So go ahead, bring home all the diabetic-friendly ingredients, put them together, blend well and enjoy them at any time of the day!

Things to Add to Your Diabetic Smoothies:

A diabetic diet is meant to keep the blood glucose level maintained all the time, so for a smoothie to be diabetic-friendly, here are the ingredients that you can use.

- **Low Glycemic Vegetables**

Vegetable greens are perfect for adding to the smoothies as they are low in sugar and high in fiber. Other than them, you can use any low-glycemic vegetable in your smoothies.

What is Low Glycemic index Value:

The Glycemic index is a scale that rates glucose with the highest value of 100 and uses it as a reference. Any food item having half of the carbs as glucose will show a Glycemic index value of 50. Veggies, fruits, and other food items with 55 or lesser glycemic index value are termed as LOW-Glycemic Index items, and they are safe to eat on a diabetic diet.

- **Low-Glycemic Fruits**

To identify fruits as diabetic-friendly, calculate or search their glycemic index value. Those who have a low GI are all good to go. Avocados, all berries, apples, pears, peaches, and grapes etc., are all good options.

- **Whole Grains**

Grains carrying more fiber are all good for diabetic patients. Whole grains and multigrain food should be added to the menu. Use brown rice instead of white. Avoid using all refined forms of wheat or grains. Grains naturally have a good amount of carbohydrates, so this fact should be kept in mind. Take only a small amount to keep your glucose levels maintained.

- **Nuts and Seeds**

Nuts and seeds are of no harm. They are enriched with special nutrients, vitamins, and all macronutrients. A small number of nuts adds a large value to the energy levels of the food.

- **Low-Fat Dairy**

Low-fat dairy is recommended on a diabetic diet, so you can use low-fat milk, plant-based milk, yoghurt, fat-free cream, or low-fat cheese to make your diabetic friendly smoothies.

- **Unsaturated Fats**

Animal fats are not at all allowed for patients suffering from type I and II diabetes as they can lead to cardiovascular diseases. You can use healthy fats if needed, such as:

- Canola oil
- Olive oil
- Sesame oil

- Grapeseed oil
- Almond butter
- Coconut butter
- Coconut oil
- Peanut oil
- Sugar-free Peanut butter
- Other vegetable oils
- Fats extracted from plant sources.

- **Low-Glycemic Sugar substitutes**

There are plenty of sugar substitutes that are carb and sugar-free. These substitutes include:

- Stevia (powdered and liquid)
- Swerve
- Xylitol
- Erythritol
- Monk fruit
- Natvia

- **Sugar-Free Flavoring, Condiments and Spices**

As long as an ingredient does not increase the carb content of a meal, it is safe to use on a diabetic diet. For store-bought condiments, read the label to confirm the glycemic index. Certain ready-made sauces carry ingredients rich in sugar like chocolate syrup or sugary apple sauce; such items have to be avoided.

- **Low-Sugar Beverages**

Try to use fresh vegetable juices, water, sugar-free almond milk, and sugar-free fruit juices in your smoothies. All the store package syrups, juices, beverages or toppings are not free from sugars, and they have to be avoided or substituted with sugar-free ones.

Things Not to Use in Diabetic Smoothies:

High carb, sugar-rich and high glycemic food are highly unhealthy for diabetic patients; therefore, a complete list of such products is necessary to keep yourself away from them. Following are the food products that are not allowed on a diabetic diet.

- **All Sugars**

Any food which has the tendency to spike the blood glucose level is not allowed on the diabetic diet. The type of sugars and sweeteners which are prohibited are as follows:

- White sugar
- Brown sugar
- Confectionary sugar
- Honey
- Molasses
- Maple syrup
- Granulated sugar

- **High Fat Dairy Products**

Dairy products like full-fat milk should not be taken on a diabetic diet plan. Other than that, all dairy products are safe to use. For cheese, look for low-fat varieties.

- **High Sodium Products**

Mainly processed foods and salt all contain sodium, and one should avoid them all. Use only the 'Unsalted' version of the food products, whether it's butter, margarine, nuts, or other items.

- **Sugary Drinks, fluids and Juices**

They can drastically increase the amount of blood glucose levels within a few minutes of drinking. So, avoid them; there are many sugar-free options available in the drinks which are suitable for diabetics. It is best to rely on homemade sugar-free drinks and beverages.

- **High Carb Vegetables**

Veggies that have a high amount of carbohydrates are not good for health. Do not add those vegetables to your grocery list like potatoes, sweet potatoes, and yams etc.

- **Sugar Syrups and Toppings**

For a diabetic diet, the patient should avoid such sugary syrups and also stay away from the sugar-rich toppings available in the stores. If you want to use them at all, trust yourself and prepare them at home with a sugar-free recipe.

- **Sweet chocolate and candies**

Sugar loaded chocolate bars and candies are extremely threatening to their health, and these all should be avoided. You can try and prepare healthy bars and candies at home with sugar-free ingredients. Go for sugar-free dark chocolate.

- **Processed Food**

Such items are loaded with preservatives, sugars, carbs, or salts; that is why they are not allowed on a diabetic diet.

- **Alcohol**

Alcohol in a very small amount is of no harm, but the regular or constant use of alcohol is bad for health and blood glucose levels. It is best not to add any alcoholic drink to your smoothies in any amount.

Diabetic Smoothies

Avocado Smoothie

Prep time: 10 minutes | Serves: 2 | Per Serving: Calories 181, Carbs 9.5g, Fat 16.1g, Protein 2.3g

Ingredients:

- Large avocado – 1, pitted and sliced

- Fresh lime juice – 1 tbsp.

- Unsweetened almond milk – 1 C.

- Coconut water – ½ C.

- Ice cubes – ¼ C.

Directions:

1) Add all the ingredients in a high-power blender and pulse until creamy.
2) Pour the smoothie into two glasses and serve immediately.

Acai Matcha Smoothie

Prep time: 10 minutes | Serves: 2 | Per Serving: Calories 288, Carbs 12g, Fat 17g, Protein 7.1g

Ingredients:

- Medium avocado – ½, pitted and sliced

- Unsweetened acai puree – 1 pack

- Almond butter – 2 tbsp.

- Matcha green tea powder – 2 tbsp.

- Liquid stevia – 4-5 drops

- Unsweetened almond milk – 1½ C.

Directions:

1) Add all the ingredients in a high-power blender and pulse until creamy.
2) Pour the smoothie into two glasses and serve immediately.

Lettuce & Spinach Smoothie

Prep time: 10 minutes |Serves: 2 | Per Serving: Calories 23, Carbs 4g, Fat 0.4g, Protein 1.6g

Ingredients:

- Romaine lettuce – 2 C., chopped

- Fresh baby spinach – 2 C.

- Fresh mint leaves – ¼ C.

- Fresh lemon juice –2 tbsp.

- Liquid stevia – 8-10 drops

- Filtered water – 1½ C.

- Ice cubes – ½ C.

Directions:

1) Add all the ingredients in a high-power blender and pulse until creamy.
2) Pour the smoothie into two glasses and serve immediately.

Green Hemp Smoothie

Prep time: 10 minutes │Serves: 2 │ Per Serving: Calories 140, Carbs 6g, Fat 12.3g, Protein 3.5g

Ingredients:

- Raw hemp seeds – 1 tbsp., shelled

- Fresh baby spinach – 2 C.

- Avocado – ½, peeled, pitted, and chopped

- Liquid stevia – 4-6 drops

- Ground cinnamon – ¼ tsp.

- Chilled filtered water – 2 C.

Directions:

1) Add all the ingredients in a high-power blender and pulse until creamy.
2) Pour the smoothie into two glasses and serve immediately.

Spinach & Coconut Smoothie

Prep time: 10 minutes | Serves: 2 | Per Serving: Calories 79, Carbs 5.3g, Fat 6.2g, Protein 2.5g

Ingredients:

- Fresh spinach – 2 C.

- Fresh ginger – 1 (1-inch) piece, peeled

- Unsweetened ground coconut – ¼ C.

- Unsweetened almond milk – 1½ C.

- Ice cubes – ¼ C.

Directions:

1) Add all the ingredients in a high-power blender and pulse until creamy.
2) Pour the smoothie into two glasses and serve immediately.

Apple, Cucumber & Spinach Smoothie

Prep time: 10 minutes | Serves: 2 | Per Serving: Calories 145, Carbs 37.4g, Fat 0.7g, Protein 2.4g

Ingredients:

- Large green apples – 2, peeled, cored, and chopped

- Fresh baby spinach – 2 C.

- Small Cucumber – 1, peeled and chopped

- Filtered water – 1½ C.

- Ice cubes – ¼ C.

Directions:

1) Add all the ingredients in a high-power blender and pulse until creamy.
2) Pour the smoothie into two glasses and serve immediately.

Spinach, Strawberry & Orange Smoothie

Prep time: 10 minutes |Serves: 2 | Per Serving: Calories 86, Carbs 19.5g,
Fat 0.6g, Protein 2.2g

Ingredients:

- Frozen strawberries – 1 C.

- Fresh spinach – 2 C.

- Fresh orange juice –1 C.

- Filtered water – 1 C.

Directions:

1) Add all the ingredients in a high-power blender and pulse until creamy.
2) Pour the smoothie into two glasses and serve immediately.

Broccoli, Kale & Apple Smoothie

Prep time: 10 minutes | Serves: 2 | Per Serving: Calories 99, Carbs 23.9g, Fat 0.3g, Protein 2.9g

Ingredients:

- Large green apple – 1, peeled, cored, and chopped
- Broccoli florets – ½ C. chopped
- Fresh kale – 2 C.
- Filtered water – 1½ C.
- Ice cubes – ¼ C.

Directions:

1) Add all the ingredients in a high-power blender and pulse until creamy.
2) Pour the smoothie into two glasses and serve immediately.

Apple, Spinach & Carrot Smoothie

Prep time: 10 minutes | Serves: 2 | Per Serving: Calories 81, Carbs 19.8g, Fat 0.4g, Protein 1.5g

Ingredients:

- Green apple – 1, peeled, cored, and chopped

- Carrot – 1, peeled and chopped

- Fresh spinach – 2 C., trimmed and chopped

- Fresh lemon juice –2 tbsp.

- Filtered water – 1½ C.

- Ice cubes – ¼ C.

Directions:

1) Add all the ingredients in a high-power blender and pulse until creamy.
2) Pour the smoothie into two glasses and serve immediately.

Kale & Avocado Smoothie

Prep time: 10 minutes | Serves: 2 | Per Serving: Calories 163, Carbs 11.3g, Fat 11g, Protein 5.3g

Ingredients:

- Fresh baby kale – 2 C.

- Avocado – ½, peeled, pitted, and chopped

- Raw hemp seeds – 1 tbsp. shelled

- Liquid stevia – 4-6 drops

- Chilled filtered water – 2 C.

Directions:

1) Add all the ingredients in a high-power blender and pulse until creamy.
2) Pour the smoothie into two glasses and serve immediately.

Spinach & Avocado Smoothie

Prep time: 10 minutes | Serves: 2 | Per Serving: Calories 153, Carbs 7.5g, Fat 13.1g, Protein 2.7g

Ingredients:

- Large avocado – ½, peeled, pitted, and chopped roughly

- Fresh spinach – 2 C.

- Liquid stevia – 2-3 drops

- Unsweetened almond milk – 1½ C.

- Ice cubes – ¼ C.

Directions:

1) Add all the ingredients in a high-power blender and pulse until creamy.
2) Pour the smoothie into two glasses and serve immediately.

Kiwi & Avocado Smoothie

Prep time: 10 minutes │Serves: 2 │ Per Serving: Calories 186, Carbs 20g, Fat 11.4g, Protein 4.2g

Ingredients:

- Kiwi –1, peeled and chopped
- Small avocado – 1, peeled, pitted, and chopped
- Cucumber – 1 C. peeled and chopped
- Fresh baby kale – 2 C.
- Fresh mint leaves – ¼ C.
- Chilled filtered water – 2 C.

Directions:

1) Add all the ingredients in a high-power blender and pulse until creamy.
2) Pour the smoothie into two glasses and serve immediately.

Matcha Chia Seed Smoothie

Prep time: 10 minutes │Serves: 2 │ Per Serving: Calories 260, Carbs 20.5g, Fat 8.2g, Protein 4.9g

Ingredients:

- Chia seeds – 2 tbsp.

- Matcha green tea powder – 2 tsp.

- Fresh lime juice –½ tsp.

- Liquid stevia – 6-8 drops

- Coconut yogurt – ¼ C.

- Unsweetened coconut milk – 1¼ C.

- Ice cubes – ¼ C.

Directions:

1) Add all the ingredients in a high-power blender and pulse until creamy.
2) Pour the smoothie into two glasses and serve immediately.

Zucchini & Spinach Smoothie

Prep time: 10 minutes | Serves: 2 | Per Serving: Calories 45, Carbs 4.8g, Fat 2.8g, Protein 1.8g

Ingredients:

- Small zucchini – 1, peeled and sliced

- Fresh spinach – ¾ C. chopped

- Ground cinnamon – 1 tsp.

- Liquid stevia – 4-6 drops

- Unsweetened almond milk – 1½ C.

- Ice cubes – ½ C.

Directions:

1) Add all the ingredients in a high-power blender and pulse until creamy.
2) Pour the smoothie into two glasses and serve immediately.

Greens & Cucumber Smoothie

Prep time: 10 minutes |Serves: 2 | Per Serving: Calories 72, Carbs 9.2g, Fat 3.8g, Protein 2.7g

Ingredients:

- Large cucumber – 1, peeled and chopped
- Fresh baby greens – 2 C.
- Fresh mint leaves – ¼ C.
- Fresh lime juice –2 tbsp.
- Chilled uunsweetened almond milk – 2 C.

Directions:

1) Add all the ingredients in a high-power blender and pulse until creamy.
2) Pour the smoothie into two glasses and serve immediately.

Avocado & Mint Smoothie

Prep time: 10 minutes | Serves: 2 | Per Serving: Calories 214, Carbs 11.7g, Fat 18.5g, Protein 3.3g

Ingredients:

- Avocado – 1, peeled, pitted, and chopped

- Fresh mint leaves – 12-14

- Fresh lime juice – 2 tbsp.

- Unsweetened almond milk – 1½ C.

- Ice cubes – ¼ C.

Directions:

1) Add all the ingredients in a high-power blender and pulse until creamy.
2) Pour the smoothie into two glasses and serve immediately.

Green Veggies Smoothie

Prep time: 10 minutes | Serves: 2 | Per Serving: Calories 19, Carbs 4.1g, Fat 0.2g, Protein 1.2g

Ingredients:

- Fresh spinach – 1 C.

- Broccoli florets – ¼ C. chopped

- Green cabbage – ¼ C. chopped

- Small green bell pepper – ½, seeded and chopped

- Liquid stevia – 8-10 drops

- Chilled filtered water – 2 C.

Directions:

1) Add all the ingredients in a high-power blender and pulse until creamy.
2) Pour the smoothie into two glasses and serve immediately.

Kale & Celery Smoothie

Prep time: 10 minutes | Serves: 2 | Per Serving: Calories 170, Carbs 13.7g, Fat 10.5g, Protein 6.8g

Ingredients:

- Fresh kale – 2 C.

- Celery stalk – 1

- Avocado – ½, peeled, pitted, and chopped

- Fresh ginger – 1 tsp. peeled and chopped

- Unsweetened almond milk – 1½ C.

- Ice cubes – ¼ C.

Directions:

1) Add all the ingredients in a high-power blender and pulse until creamy.
2) Pour the smoothie into two glasses and serve immediately.

Cucumber, Ginger & Parsley Smoothie

Prep time: 10 minutes | Serves: 2 | Per Serving: Calories 44, Carbs 8.5g, Fat 0.8g, Protein 2.7g

Ingredients:

- Cucumber – 2 C. peeled and chopped

- Fresh parsley – 2 C.

- Fresh ginger – 1 (1-inch) piece, peeled and chopped

- Fresh lemon juice – 2 tbsp.

- Liquid stevia – 4-6 drops

- Chilled filtered water – 2 C.

Directions:

1) Add all the ingredients in a high-power blender and pulse until creamy.
2) Pour the smoothie into two glasses and serve immediately.

Kale & Cucumber Smoothie

Prep time: 10 minutes | Serves: 2 | Per Serving: Calories 84, Carbs 10.7g, Fat 4.1g, Protein 4.7g

Ingredients:

- Green spirulina powder – 2 tsp.

- Fresh kale – 1½ C.

- Cucumber – 1 C. peeled and chopped

- Chia seeds – 1 tbsp.

- Unsweetened almond milk – 1½ C.

- Ice cubes – ¼ C.

Directions:

1) Add all the ingredients in a high-power blender and pulse until creamy.
2) Pour the smoothie into two glasses and serve immediately.

Cucumber & Lettuce Smoothie

Prep time: 10 minutes | Serves: 2 | Per Serving: Calories 92, Carbs 19.1g, Fat 1g, Protein 3.8g

Ingredients:

- Cucumber – 1, peeled and chopped
- Lettuce leaves – 1 C.
- Fresh mint leaves – ½ C.
- Fresh ginger – 1 tbsp. grated
- Fresh lime juice – 1 tbsp.
- Liquid stevia – 2-3 drops
- Coconut water – 2 C.
- Ice cubes – ¼ C.

Directions:

1) Add all the ingredients in a high-power blender and pulse until creamy.
2) Pour the smoothie into two glasses and serve immediately.

Minty Greens Smoothie

Prep time: 10 minutes | Serves: 2 | Per Serving: Calories 195, Carbs 13.8g, Fat 16.2g, Protein 5.1g

Ingredients:

- Avocado – ½, peeled, pitted, and chopped

- Fresh kale – 1 C.

- Small cucumber – ½, peeled and chopped

- Fresh mint leaves – ¼ C.

- Almond butter – 1 tbsp.

- Fresh lemon juice – 1 tbsp.

- Unsweetened almond milk – 1¼ C.

- Ice cubes – ½ C.

Directions:

1) Add all the ingredients in a high-power blender and pulse until creamy.
2) Pour the smoothie into two glasses and serve immediately.

Cucumber & Mint Smoothie

Prep time: 10 minutes │Serves: 2 │ Per Serving: Calories 78, Carbs 11.7g,
Fat 3g, Protein 3.2g

Ingredients:

- Large cucumber – 1, peeled and chopped

- Fresh kale – 1 C.

- Fresh mint leaves – ¼ C.

- Fresh lemon juice – 2 tbsp.

- Unsweetened almond milk – 1½ C.

- Ice cubes – ¼ C.

Directions:

1) Add all the ingredients in a high-power blender and
   pulse until creamy.
2) Pour the smoothie into two glasses and serve
   immediately.

Avocado, Mint & Lemon Smoothie

Prep time: 10 minutes │Serves: 2 │ Per Serving: Calories 186, Carbs 2.6g, Fat 16.7g, Protein 9g

Ingredients:

- Avocado – 1 peeled, pitted and chopped

- Fresh mint leaves – 12-14

- Fresh lemon juice – 2 tbsp.

- Vanilla extract – ½ tsp.

- Unsweetened almond milk – 1½ C.

- Ice cubes – ¼ C.

Directions:

1) Add all the ingredients in a high-power blender and pulse until creamy.
2) Pour the smoothie into two glasses and serve immediately.

Avocado, Kale & Celery Smoothie

Prep time: 10 minutes |Serves: 2 | Per Serving: Calories 167, Carbs 11.2g, Fat 13.6g, Protein 3.5g

Ingredients:

- Fresh kale – 2 C. chopped

- Celery stalks – 1-2, chopped

- Avocado – ½, peeled, pitted, and chopped

- Fresh ginger – 1 (½-inch) piece, chopped

- Fresh turmeric root – 1 (½-inch) piece, chopped

- Chilled unsweetened almond milk – 2 C.

Directions:

1) Add all the ingredients in a high-power blender and pulse until creamy.
2) Pour the smoothie into two glasses and serve immediately.

Grapes & Avocado Smoothie

Prep time: 10 minutes | Serves: 2 | Per Serving: Calories 240, Carbs 26.4g, Fat 17.3g, Protein 1.9g

Ingredients:

- Seedless green grapes – 1¼ C.

- Small avocado – 1, peeled, pitted, and chopped

- Liquid stevia – 2-3 drops

- Green tea – 2 C. Brewed and Cooled

Directions:

1) Add all the ingredients in a high-power blender and pulse until creamy.
2) Pour the smoothie into two glasses and serve immediately.

Kiwi & Cucumber Smoothie

Prep time: 10 minutes | Serves: 2 | Per Serving: Calories 94, Carbs 22.6g, Fat 0.8g, Protein 3g

Ingredients:

- Kiwis – 2, peeled and chopped
- Small cucumbers – 2, peeled and chopped
- Fresh parsley leaves – 2 tbsp.
- Fresh ginger – ½ tsp. chopped
- Chilled filtered water – 1½ C.

Directions:

1) Add all the ingredients in a high-power blender and pulse until creamy.
2) Pour the smoothie into two glasses and serve immediately.

Spinach, Apple & Pear Smoothie

Prep time: 10 minutes │Serves: 2 │ Per Serving: Calories 131, Carbs 36.2g, Fat 0.5g, Protein 2g

Ingredients:

- Small apples – 2, peeled, cored, and sliced

- Small pears – 2, peeled, cored, and sliced

- Fresh spinach – 3 C.

- Chilled organic coconut water – 1 C.

- Chilled filtered water – 1 C.

Directions:

1) Add all the ingredients in a high-power blender and pulse until creamy.
2) Pour the smoothie into two glasses and serve immediately.

Cucumber, Greens & Herbs Smoothie

Prep time: 10 minutes | Serves: 2 | Per Serving: Calories 60, Carbs 11.4g, Fat 0.6g, Protein 2.5g

Ingredients:

- Large cucumber – 1, peeled and chopped
- Mixed fresh greens – 2 C.
- Lettuce – ½ C.
- Fresh parsley leaves – ¼ C.
- Fresh mint Leaves – ¼ C.
- Liquid stevia – 2-3 drops
- Fresh lime juice – 1 tbsp.
- Filtered water – 1½ C.
- Ice cubes – ¼ C.

Directions:

1) Add all the ingredients in a high-power blender and pulse until creamy.
2) Pour the smoothie into two glasses and serve immediately.

Carrot & Apple Smoothie

Prep time: 10 minutes | Serves: 2 | Per Serving: Calories 145, Carbs 37.1g, Fat 0.5g, Protein 1.2g

Ingredients:

- Large green apples – 2, peeled, cored, and chopped

- Carrots – 2, peeled and chopped

- Fresh lemon juice – 2 tbsp.

- Filtered water – 1½ C.

- Ice cubes – ¼ C.

Directions:

1) Add all the ingredients in a high-power blender and pulse until creamy.
2) Pour the smoothie into two glasses and serve immediately.

Raspberry, Cabbage & Tomato Smoothie

Prep time: 10 minutes |Serves: 2 | Per Serving: Calories 70, Carbs 16.9g, Fat 0.5g, Protein 1.6g

Ingredients:

- Fresh raspberries – 1 C.

- Red cabbage – 1 C. chopped

- Small tomato – 1, chopped

- Filtered water –1½ C.

- Ice cubes – ¼ C.

Directions:

1) Add all the ingredients in a high-power blender and pulse until creamy.
2) Pour the smoothie into two glasses and serve immediately.

Carrot, Tomato & Celery Smoothie

Prep time: 10 minutes | Serves: 2 | Per Serving: Calories 62, Carbs 13.6g, Fat 0.6g, Protein 2.6g

Ingredients:

- Medium tomatoes – 4

- Large carrot – 1, peeled and chopped

- Celery stalk – 1, chopped

- Liquid stevia – 2-4 drops

- Fresh lemon juice – 2 tsp.

- Filtered water – 2 C.

- Ice cubes – ¼ C.

Directions:

1) Add all the ingredients in a high-power blender and pulse until creamy.
2) Pour the smoothie into two glasses and serve immediately.

Pumpkin Smoothie

Prep time: 10 minutes | Serves: 2 | Per Serving: Calories 171, Carbs 6.7g, Fat 3.3g, Protein 19.8g

Ingredients:

- Canned sugar-free pumpkin – 1 C.

- Unsweetened protein powder – ½ C.

- Stevia powder – ¼-½ tsp.

- Pumpkin pie spice – ½ tsp.

- Vanilla extract – 1 tsp.

- Unsweetened almond milk – 2 C.

- Ice cubes – ¼ C.

Directions:

1) Add all the ingredients in a high-power blender and pulse until creamy.
2) Pour the smoothie into two glasses and serve immediately.

Blueberry & Pear Smoothie

Prep time: 10 minutes | Serves: 2 | Per Serving: Calories 192, Carbs 34.7g, Fat 6.2g, Protein 3.6g

Ingredients:

- Large pears – 2, peeled, cored, and chopped

- Frozen blueberries – 1 C.

- Raw cashews – 2 tbsp.

- Hemp seeds – 1 tbsp.

- Filtered water – 1¼ C.

Directions:

1) Add all the ingredients in a high-power blender and pulse until creamy.
2) Pour the smoothie into two glasses and serve immediately.

Orange Smoothie

Prep time: 10 minutes | Serves: 2 | Per Serving: Calories 106, Carbs 22.6g, Fat 2g, Protein 2.2g

Ingredients:

- Medium oranges – 2, peeled, seeded, and sectioned
- Liquid stevia – 2-3 drops
- Unsweetened almond milk – 1 C.
- Ice cubes – ¼ C.

Directions:

1) Add all the ingredients in a high-power blender and pulse until creamy.
2) Pour the smoothie into two glasses and serve immediately.

Vanilla Smoothie

Prep time: 10 minutes | Serves: 2 | Per Serving: Calories 197, Carbs 8.6g, Fat 6.6g, Protein 24g

Ingredients:

- Unsweetened vanilla protein powder – ½ C.

- Almond butter – 2 tbsp.

- Vanilla extract – 2 tsp.

- Liquid stevia – 6-8 drops

- Chilled unsweetened almond milk – 2 C.

Directions:

1) Add all the ingredients in a high-power blender and pulse until creamy.
2) Pour the smoothie into two glasses and serve immediately.

Cranberry Smoothie

Prep time: 10 minutes | Serves: 2 | Per Serving: Calories 188, Carbs 29.9g, Fat 3.3g, Protein 8.5g

Ingredients:

- Fresh cranberries – 2 C.

- Vanilla extract – 1 tsp.

- Liquid stevia – 3-4 drops

- Unsweetened almond milk – 1¼ C.

- Ice cubes – ½ C.

Directions:

1) Add all the ingredients in a high-power blender and pulse until creamy.
2) Pour the smoothie into two glasses and serve immediately.

Cherry Smoothie

Prep time: 10 minutes | Serves: 2 | Per Serving: Calories 120, Carbs 23.6g, Fat 2.6g, Protein 2.8g

Ingredients:

- Fresh cherries – 2 C. pitted
- Pinch of ground cinnamon
- Liquid stevia – 3-4 drops
- Unsweetened almond milk – 1½ C.
- Ice cubes – ½ C.

Directions:

1) Add all the ingredients in a high-power blender and pulse until creamy.
2) Pour the smoothie into two glasses and serve immediately.

Pear & Apple Smoothie

Prep time: 10 minutes |Serves: 2 | Per Serving: Calories 194, Carbs 37.1g, Fat 3.3g, Protein 7.8g

Ingredients:

- Large pear – 1, peeled, cored, and sliced
- Large green apple – 1, peeled, cored, and sliced
- Almonds – 2 tbsp. chopped
- Vanilla extract – ¼ tsp.
- Fat-Free Milk – 1½ C.
- Ice cubes – ¼ C.

Directions:

1) Add all the ingredients in a high-power blender and pulse until creamy.
2) Pour the smoothie into two glasses and serve immediately.

Peach, Apricot & Carrot Smoothie

Prep time: 10 minutes │Serves: 2 │ Per Serving: Calories 105, Carbs 24.7g, Fat 0.9g, Protein 2.6g

Ingredients:

- Apricots – 4, pitted and chopped

- Peaches – 2, pitted and chopped

- Medium carrot – 1, peeled and chopped

- Filtered water – 1½ C.

- Ice cubes – ¼ C.

Directions:

1) Add all the ingredients in a high-power blender and pulse until creamy.
2) Pour the smoothie into two glasses and serve immediately.

Blackberry & Spinach Smoothie

Prep time: 10 minutes | Serves: 2 | Per Serving: Calories 97, Carbs 9.1g, Fat 5.8g, Protein 4.8g

Ingredients:

- Fresh blackberries – ¾ C.

- Fresh spinach – 2 C.

- Fresh mint leaves – ¼ C.

- Sunflower seeds – 1 tbsp.

- Pumpkin seeds – 1 tbsp.

- Unsweetened almond milk – 1½ C.

- Ice cubes – ¼ C.

Directions:

1) Add all the ingredients in a high-power blender and pulse until creamy.
2) Pour the smoothie into two glasses and serve immediately.

Strawberries & Orange Smoothie

Prep time: 10 minutes | Serves: 2 | Per Serving: Calories 153, Carbs 35.5g, Fat 1.2g, Protein 1.2g

Ingredients:

- Fresh strawberries – 1¼ C. hulled and sliced

- Fresh raspberries – 1¼ C.

- Liquid stevia – 3-4 drops

- Fresh orange juice – 1½ C.

- Ice cubes – ¼ C.

Directions:

1) Add all the ingredients in a high-power blender and pulse until creamy.
2) Pour the smoothie into two glasses and serve immediately.

Papaya Smoothie

Prep time: 10 minutes | Serves: 2 | Per Serving: Calories 82, Carbs 16.7g, Fat 2.2g, Protein 1.2g

Ingredients:

- Papaya – 2 C. peeled and sliced

- Unsweetened almond milk – 1 C.

- Ice cubes – ½ C.

Directions:

1) Add all the ingredients in a high-power blender and pulse until creamy.
2) Pour the smoothie into two glasses and serve immediately.

Strawberry & Spinach Smoothie

Prep time: 10 minutes │Serves: 2 │ Per Serving: Calories 70, Carbs 9.7g, Fat 2.9g, Protein 2g

Ingredients:

- Fresh spinach – 2½ C.

- Frozen strawberries – 1¼ C.

- Unsweetened almond milk – 1½ C.

Directions:

1) Add all the ingredients in a high-power blender and pulse until creamy.
2) Pour the smoothie into two glasses and serve immediately.

Strawberry, Cucumber & Greens Smoothie

Prep time: 10 minutes | Serves: 2 | Per Serving: Calories 84, Carbs 13.8g, Fat 3g, Protein 3.2g

Ingredients:

- Fresh strawberries – 1 C. hulled and sliced

- Fresh kale – 1 C.

- Fresh spinach – 1 C.

- Cucumber – ½, peeled and chopped

- Unsweetened almond milk – 1½ C.

- Ice cubes – ¼ C.

Directions:

1) Add all the ingredients in a high-power blender and pulse until creamy.
2) Pour the smoothie into two glasses and serve immediately.

Strawberry & Water –melon Smoothie

Prep time: 10 minutes │ Serves: 2 │ Per Serving: Calories 113, Carbs 19.7g, Fat 3.6g, Protein 2.4g

Ingredients:

- Fresh watermelon – 1½ C. seeded and cubed

- Frozen strawberries – 1½ C.

- Hemp seeds – 1 tbsp.

- Fresh lime juice – 2 tbsp.

- Unsweetened almond milk – 1 C.

Directions:

1) Add all the ingredients in a high-power blender and pulse until creamy.
2) Pour the smoothie into two glasses and serve immediately.

Berries & Yogurt Smoothie

Prep time: 10 minutes | Serves: 2 | Per Serving: Calories 206, Carbs 34.4g, Fat 2.1g, Protein 8.6g

Ingredients:

- Frozen mixed berries – 1½ C.

- Vanilla extract – ½ tsp.

- Plain yogurt – 1 C.

- Fresh orange juice – 1 C.

- Ice cubes – ¼ C.

Directions:

1) Add all the ingredients in a high-power blender and pulse until creamy.
2) Pour the smoothie into two glasses and serve immediately.

Berries, Kale & Avocado Smoothie

Prep time: 10 minutes | Serves: 2 | Per Serving: Calories 188, Carbs 29.9g, Fat 3.3g, Protein 8.5g

Ingredients:

- Frozen blueberries – ½ C.

- Fresh raspberries – ½ C.

- Fresh kale – 1 C.

- Avocado – ½, peeled, pitted, and chopped

- Green spirulina powder – ½ tsp.

- Unsweetened almond milk – 2 C.

Directions:

1) Add all the ingredients in a high-power blender and pulse until creamy.
2) Pour the smoothie into two glasses and serve immediately.

Cherry & Blueberry Smoothie

Prep time: 10 minutes | Serves: 2 | Per Serving: Calories 188, Carbs 29.9g, Fat 3.3g, Protein 8.5g

Ingredients:

- Frozen blueberries – 1¼ C.

- Frozen unsweetened cherries – 1 C.

- Fat-free plain yogurt – 6 oz.

- Unsweetened almond milk – 1 C.

Directions:

1) Add all the ingredients in a high-power blender and pulse until creamy.
2) Pour the smoothie into two glasses and serve immediately.

Blackberry Smoothie

Prep time: 10 minutes | Serves: 2 | Per Serving: Calories 164, Carbs 32.8g, Fat 1g, Protein 6.9g

Ingredients:

- Fresh Blackberries – 2 C.
- Vanilla Extract – ¼ tsp.
- Fresh orange juice – 1 C.
- Fat-free milk – 1 C.
- Ice cubes – ¼ C.

Directions:

1) Add all the ingredients in a high-power blender and pulse until creamy.
2) Pour the smoothie into two glasses and serve immediately.

Conclusion

So, are you ready to try out all the low-glycemic ingredients in your smoothies? All the 50 smoothies in this cookbook are extremely healthy, and they are a perfect way to add a variety of nutritious veggies and other food items to your daily menu without having to put extra effort into cooking. So, go ahead, try one each day and enjoy!

Made in the USA
Middletown, DE
23 October 2023

41289817R00036